DECADES
Selected Poems

Decades

✝

Selected Poems

Joseph Massey

THE EXILE PRESS
2024

Joseph Massey, *Decades*
First published in 2024
by The Exile Press

ISBN: 9798880299560

Typeset *&* design: Gerry Cambridge

© Joseph Massey 2024

Contents

Prologue • 11

from *Areas of Fog*

Poem Including History • 21
Conversation • 22
Wait • 23
Listening to Joseph Ceravolo's
    Home Recordings • 24
Conditions • 25
Autumnal Equinox • 26
Lost Coast • 27
Property Line • 29
Samoa Peninsula Jetty • 36
Arcata Marsh • 37
On a False Spring • 38

from *At the Point*

The Process • 41
Close • 42
No Name Pond • 43
Exit North • 44
A Line Made by Walking • 45
Notice • 48
Forming • 49
From a Window • 50

Prescription • 61
No Vehicles Beyond this Point • 62
Elk Ridge • 63

from *To Keep Time*

Another Rehearsal for Morning • 67
An Undisclosed Location in
    Northern California • 68
Surround • 75
Passage • 76
Other Increments • 77
Anchoritic • 78
Microclimate(s) • 79
Gone • 87
Wrack Zone • 88

from *Illocality*

Turned • 93
After Wittgenstein • 94
Route 31 • 95
The Frame • 96
A Title For the Haze • 97
Curtains • 98
On Migration • 99
Take Place • 100
Polar Low • 105
Contain • 106
Gauge • 108
Illocality • 109

from *A New Silence*

> For the Margin • 115
> The Reprieve • 116
> Present Conditions • 118
> Late March • 119
> Vigil • 120
> Otherwise • 121
> Temple • 122
> Brookside • 123
> On the Solstice • 124
> An Offering • 125
> Nothing More • 126
> Clear • 127
> The Work • 128
> The Practice • 129
> Garden Level • 131
> Placeholder • 134
> Northern Tracks • 135
> After Trakl • 139
> A Window in New England • 140

from *Rosary Made of Air*

> Breath Work • 151
> Manifesto • 161
> The Shape of Something Said • 166
> Late Time • 168
> Keepsake • 171
> Poem Against Cancellation • 172
> To a New Friend • 174
> Satori in Easthampton • 175

September 8th, 2021 • 176
Altar and Offering • 178
On the Cusp • 191
The Turn • 200
The Walk • 201
Removed • 202

from *The Light of No Other Hour*

Soma • 205
Intercession • 206
Spear Thistle • 208
Closer to October • 209
Far • 210
Deep November • 211
Found Poem • 212
Before Mass • 219
Pilgrim (On the Feast Day of
    St. Benedict Joseph Labre) • 220
Saint Brigid's • 221
Prayer Walk • 222
Beads • 223
Lux Brumalis • 229
Three Mornings in March • 237
Lenten Syllables • 240
Unseasonably • 245
The Last Poem • 247

Acknowledgements • 251
About the Author • 251
A NOTE ON THE TYPES • 252

*For the friends, in art and life,
who remain steadfast*

Gloria in Excelsis Deo

Prologue

i.

Beneath morning's gray, lopsided
ceiling, I grip the air for balance.
Air like glass in fragments—
the frigid drizzle. Walking,
I hold a prayer in mind, not
repeating, but breathing
each word anew.
I pass the lawn
with the dead sunflowers
(their black, caved-in faces)
and tomatoes heavy with rot—
vines sagging toward the sidewalk.
Chalk drawings faded by rain:
mangled stick men
and slogans smeared illegible.
Like the mind without prayer.
Like the mind without prayer
to resolve the shattered sound
of the animal I am.

ii.

Is this the season
to sleep off disease,
bunker under
a low frequency,
and write
into the distance
between shadows
on leaf-calloused lawns?

*

First heard
and then seen:
a bedraggled formation
of geese
palpitating south
in a low-slung sky.

*

Late autumn mist, all
that penetrates: a porch light
and church bells chiming.

iii.

Morning haze burning off—
the cross
on the steeple gleams.

*

Starlings (one mind
radiating throughout
a thousand wings)
contract and expand
over a vacant church
like a plastic bag
whipped by wind.

*

Red as a warning,
a winterberry shrub
flashes through the gaps
between coils
of dormant grapevines.

*

In the dying light
a yellow leaf
clings.

iv.

Snow in slow streaks
animates
a skeletal tree.
Quiet enough now
to hear
the heavy flakes
landing
on a pile of leaves.

*

Into a vortex
of dead leaves—
vivid red
and yellow—
the day evaporates.

*

On the other side
of an impassable patch
of woods cut through by
a creek, I see a steeple
and the cross caught up in fog.

*

A patch of moss
on a stone wall
like a lantern lit

with the last light.

*

At empire's end, I
watch sparrows
rip apart the bread
thrown across a lawn.

V.

First Sunday of Advent

Inexplicably, the scent of jasmine
threads the night air. Cold air.
Closer now to winter than the depths of fall.
Nothing's in bloom but a dumpster
overflowing, and a few chimneys—
it must be the woodsmoke that thins
into imagined jasmine. Walking home,
streetlights dim, I see as far as I can think.
And here the season begins, in the dark,
waiting for the Word to emerge
like the amber glow
in a window at the end of the road.

vi.

After the snow squall
white absorbs blue
under dusk.

And lamplit windows
suspended
in the drift

of things receding—

how they signal life.
Company
and compass

in the gathering black.

vii.

    The new morning:
a shattered gull cry
fading behind closed eyes.
    White light beats through
half-closed blinds.

    What needs to be said
says itself in weather,
and the breath
    before a first word is uttered.

    And when a word arrives,
may it be vacant
and weightless on the tongue—
    a small vessel for awe.

from *Areas of Fog*

Poem Including History

A curb the color
of nausea.
Parking lot gravel

splintered with glass,
dog shit, receipts.
Storage sheds—a row

of lamp-lit doors
deepening
as dusk thickens. Now,

night, they're all that's left
and traffic's
excuse for music

moving through the room.

Conversation

Horizon
bound by

road signs
and wires.

Low tide:
wide swaths

of mud
rub in.

Words, we
have none.

We're lost
in the tone

splayed
between

shadows
bending

with the
wind's pitch.

Wait

Inside
a power line's

slack
center, the

afternoon
moon, half

full, is a
dent.

Listening to Joseph Ceravolo's Home Recordings

In the room
of a memory

of a room.
Static

brackets each
syllable.

Afternoon
effaces the floor

while the
pills take

effect.
All I will

amount to:
the hours

these walls
enclose

as song.

Conditions

Haze, chalk dust
white, replaces
the space I

realize as
sky. Forests far
off, not too far,

on fire—so
goes the word
and this evidence.

Autumnal Equinox

Sober for once, for what—
for the words to budge.

We spent summer propped up
by each other's stuttering.

There are seasons here
if you squint. And there's

relief in the landscape's
sloughed off cusps of color

fallen over the familiar
landmarks, the familiar

trash—things that last.

Lost Coast

A cragged stack
in the gathering gray
surf, crowded by
seabirds,
their prehistoric
profiles. We
pull over
to argue, not
to talk,
but the words
won't form—
the terrain
overtakes them.
Bright litter
drifts into
sand and
small stones
at our feet.
Across the
street, cows
corral behind
barbed wire,
stock-still
in each other's
shadows. We
don't need words
to read the sun's

angle. We know
it will soon be
too dim
to navigate
the switchbacks
without guardrails
we descended
to arrive.

Property Line

Hill's red
tethered
edge—

berries
that numbed
your tongue.

★

Eucalyptus
limbs lisp

wind winds
off the bay.

★

Mosquitoes
dusk tugs
from the lawn

reflect against
the clenched
fuchsia buds.

*

Swallows
whisk the rifts

dusk dims
between leaves

on the tree
whose name

I refuse to find.

*

Factory lights
crease night's
farthest seam

where hills
daub black
deeper than

the black en-
compassing.

*

Next
door's
flower's

scent
parts
the curtain.

*

Flies, sun-
dried, line
the windowsill.

Measure
what was summer.

*

Hummingbird
through a vortex of gnats
navigates nasturtiums

                unraveled
        over a gravel path.

*

Honeysuckle
scent like
an open vowel

wrung out
in the rain's
gloss-

olalia.

*

Spider web
(wind-
ripped)

weighted with
a wet receipt.

*

Fog torn
around
a crow

rowing
toward
a row of

eucalyptus.

★

These interruptions

of color
in the overgrowth.

★

Wing-slur—
half a humming-

bird's body
swallowed by

one of the few
fuchsias left.

★

This dusk-
colored
landscape

the rain

deepens

into night.

*

Power lines
dent the dawn.

What words I
woke with

dissolve.

*

Enough to make
the foliage
flinch,

wind slits.

Music sifts

out of a house.

Samoa Peninsula Jetty

Dead barnacles and gull shit grip the driftwood.

Your voice ahead of me. I stop to watch

the surf's thrown foam spot the rocks.

A buoy clangs against the downswell.

Arcata Marsh

       Mudscape—tide's out—
out as far as fog gives sight.

       Periphery-flecked,
orange-white
lichen latched to limbs

       I thought were your
fingers—
       your face turned
back by wind.

On a False Spring

The names
we don't
remember, how

they flower—
smeared along
the field's

edge—
beyond our
mouths.

from *At the Point*

The Process

Cross-stitched
outside sounds
double the day's

indoor confusion.
How to untwine
noise, to see.

There's the bay,
highway slashed
beneath; water

a weaker shade
of gray than this
momentary sky's

widening bruise.
The page turns
on the table, bare

despite all
I thought was
written there.

Close

Hedges
dredged in
shadow, where

a song's
confusion
roosts, tell

the time.

No Name Pond

Attached to blackberry thorns
a plastic bag balloons

beside a faded sign:
NO ARTIFICIAL LURES.

Insects click
in brick and wood—

a kind of metronome
my mind stumbles to.

Exit North

Exhaust shrouds
a shrub in bloom
on the corner, too
distant to discern
its color. Red
graffiti underscores
a sign that points north.
March—spring singes
the sky's organized
incisions. Plastic
drifts into hydrangeas.
The pause before
one perception
extinguishes another,
extinguishes nostalgia.
Late winter waste
clumped shallow over grates.

A Line Made by Walking

Humid June
air that barely

moves, and yet
the water in the

creek wrinkles,
pushed around

fronds and
broken bottle,

or is it
chipped quartz

trapping the
glare. Rusted

shed at the road's
shoulder falls back

into flowering
brush falling over

the hill's edge.
Train tracks, grass-

smothered, run
behind it. A crow

collects trash
from a strip-

mall parking lot,
carries it to the

church roof,
then claps off

to collect more
as a gnat—no

a floater in
my right eye

bobs back and forth.
Traffic's sustained

sibilance grows
louder later. Still

the sun's white,
the haze is

white, the air
is locked

in it, and I
squint, and lean

into it, as if
to find

a word there.

Notice

By the parking lot
of a house
emptied after foreclosure,
a yellow-jacket

slinks
through curved rain
into a half-opened fuchsia—
both heavy with water.

Forming

The languages
we dream—

their dissolution
into morning's

striations,
what scores

the contours
of the room

we find ourselves
breathing in—

how they leave us
without speech,

in pieces—a part
of the pattern

day consumes
to become.

From a Window

> *The shadow does not move.*
> —William Carlos Williams

i.

Day ascends into day,
and last night's
vocabulary
is lost.

Through the bone
of a stutter

lodged in my throat,
to somehow say
what wants to be said.

Say it.

Black moth
wrecked
against glass.

Cactus aglow
on a narrow ledge.

ii.

Between
a bulk of clouds

broken
over dawn

blackbirds
disperse.

Page
as white
as the sun.

iii.

This year's
      first few
rhododendrons

      hover above
purple and orange
      flowers I

can't find
      in the field guide.

iv.

Paint can
        half-sunk
in dried mud

        full of yesterday's
                rain.

v.

Lit amber by
back door light

a skunk prowls
bramble's edge

—blackberry vines
and dandelions

bunched alongside
the garage—

into alley's black
spilling moths.

vi.

Weeds after
days of rain
and fog
curve

from one end
of the sidewalk
to the other

above snails crushed
last night
while walking home
drunk in the dark.

vii.

In vines'

leaves
latticed over
the sunk shed roof

gnats or bees
—both—blur.

viii.

Over the window
        cobwebs
embody a breeze
        neither of us feel.

ix.

Gibbous moon
splinters

past bare
fuchsia branches

and my face
cast

on lamp-glared
glass.

x.

Dawn skims the blinds
into a shape   shadows

—children, traffic, pigeons
cut across—

> What's left of the dream:
> a hole in my head
>
> the dreamed words
> draw through and decompose.

xi.

The hills
aligned

with clouds
aligned

with the
windowsill

levitate.

Prescription

To think through
each word's
particular weather.

To stand
just far enough
outside of the page.

A field drapes
the eye
in limitless revision.

How shadows
that fill the gap
between two stones

imply the sky's weight.

No Vehicles Beyond this Point

Tape unspools from a cassette,
        collects—a nest—between two
pieces of driftwood, measures
        the wind's direction. Wind pinched
with skunk, sea salt, gasoline.

Elk Ridge

Night seeps
into its name.

At the edge
where black

oak clouds
an embankment

what I imagined
was silence

becomes enough
music for now—

the constellated
sounds

nouns

from *To Keep Time*

Another Rehearsal for Morning

Beyond a hand
held beyond itself
the mist is too thick to see.
A dream fragment (a phrase
I wanted to remember)
goes mute in this—
extinguished. Call it
consciousness. What
we lose to recover.
Acacia branches bend
the hill's edge
off-orange. A blur,
a deeper blur.
A clarity I can't carry.

An Undisclosed Location in Northern California

i.

Over a gorge flanked
by black oak
ravens relay calls

that double back in
echo. Thick
morning thinned to a

pitch of sun and no
hangover.
Here you're either lost

or lost. A wordless-
ness written
into the dirt writes

itself around you.

ii.

Wire-mesh fence—from
this angle—
quarters the daylit

quarter moon.

iii.

As long as blood runs
the body,
there is no silence.

Silence hums. A sound.
The sound of
next to nothing—no-

thing—under our skin.

iv.

Parenthetical
pampas grass
shrouds a used condom

in useless shadow.

v.

Information plaque
words worn to
glyphs. Jagged weather—

gouged-out cliff ledge clutched
by bramble-
fused shrubs. Vertigo

holds my body here.

vi.

A fog bank fastens
horizon
to horizon. Names

unfold the field. My
mind is lapped
and lost in it. Lapped

and lost in this slow
flowering
of form flowering

out of form.

vii.

World no more a world
than thinking
allows, and the light

bound here in its place.

Surround

Three weeks of rain.
The wreckage glitters.

A cold front culls other colors: look
long enough and the brush becomes
another hill or mountain, cloud

crowding skyline.
The mind

brought past its racket
swallows each gradation.

A private speech, a season.

Passage

Cold, yet
the page radiates
with what night can't condense.
Call it

winter, this
wracked interior
no light lifts.
Hail,

a sudden
gust, throttles
the ceiling
as if to describe it.

Other Increments

Winter's arrhythmic timbre
dislocates landscape, con-
jures robins where frost

and mud would be.
This supposed January.
No rain to fail to say

the hours through: the din,
the dumbshow, the light
off-kilter and hollowing.

How everyday ready-mades
anchor the real. Acacia
blooms—migraine-yellow—

approach the window.
Turn. Find tide's out:
black plane beneath water's

holographic gray.
Cloud-rifts rove.
Three bees drone

around the sill
as if to carve their form
from warped wood.

Anchoritic

Listening to wind
dislodge objects
in the dark around
my room, I want
to think thinking
is enough to locate
a world, but it isn't.
It isn't this one.
It isn't this world,
weather.

Microclimate(s)

> *Ecstasy evolves slowly*
> *within*
> *a closed horizon. . .*
>
> —Pam Rehm

i.

Place,
placed apart.

Sun scrapes hills—
an outline

wedged in
white, off-white.

    (The limits
delineate particulars.)

Tide gone
out, shore

pocked, mud
balked with debris.

Weeds saturated black
tangle between

barnacle-
crusted pylons.

The near-silence
rattles me

to attention.
Nest of stone

foam-slapped.
Something

lifts, settles
on the water:

a name,
a nonsense syllable.

ii.

The air itself dismantled
thread by braided
thread.

    Shadows fall farther
from what they fail to copy.

I squint
to hear the ocean
pierce an aperture
in sky

not wide enough
for words—

even a word—
to escape.

iii.

No time to think
or speak when sky
cleaves rain and sun
filtered through stacked
clouds, a kind of kaleidoscope
you can't imagine as California
imagines it: the scale
disrupts the ordinary borders:
edges the eye holds to
flake off in shade
wavering   as an eddy.

A vividness
leaves you beside yourself.

iv.

Rain stops, things
shattered
mend.

A split minute
of blindness
before objects
take shape.
Field's
furrowed
gradations

no palette
or pixel
could conjure.
And now wind

picks up,
snagging
the glare—

the glare
snagging
wind.

v.

Season signaled by webs

clasped or partial-
ly clasped to
shadowed gaps

visible
when a thread's glint
snags an eye and

captures how round the sun

cuts
between houses.

vi.

Bewilder-
ment persists
in this persistent
pressure gradient.
What I want to say
I can't see to say

I can't see to say it.

Hills twine power lines
now that the sky cracks
to let some-
thing other than

its own
involution
through.

vii.

Ripped thin stratus
gives a false horizon

      No room for music
when weather walls thought.

To find a way to live
with the gray—
is the thing. To walk
without rut or ledge; to track

through static. To stop looking
      as if looking
were a way out.

Gone

Some evidence
of a world
raw to my waking, word-

      less at first, re-
coils into noise—

Name it summer,

an after-
thought,
a hangover.

A monkey flower

                flung
over its own shadow.

Wrack Zone

It's the ocean
sounding out

a panic
I otherwise

couldn't
pronounce.

Ouroboric
vowel fixed

to a low sky's
loop of

variable white.

•

Decayed
rope of

bull-head
kelp

distends
from tide-

tamped
sand.

Mind
mirrors

that surface,
shape,

the moment
I imagine

if I thought
far enough

I'd leave my
face.

from *Illocality*

Turned

A notch
at the top of the mountain—

the eye
without a thought

threads the sky through.

How hours take

the stain of hours
and hold beneath their bloom

these things arranged
to resemble a season.

Summer's hum and lag.

To walk into it—

breathe the frequencies
that knot the air, another

animal baffled
to be an animal.

After Wittgenstein

      A contrail divides the skyline
wrinkled with heat. Flies circle trash—
      clear plastic—at the seam
between brick path and lawn.
      Hours atrophy.

      There is the inexpressible
but it doesn't show itself
      today. It doesn't
show itself in summer.

      Even shade as it erases
radiates.

Route 31

Yellow center-line
split with roadkill.

First day of summer—I've got my omen—

the clouds are hollow, roving
above a parking lot.

Each strip mall pennant blurred.

So much metal
shoving sun

the sun shoves back.

The Frame

Morning makes
shapes, re-
combines the
room. A blue
line over
a gray line—
the slippage
pinned to
a wall.
What the window
lets in.
What it lets out.
Weather
moving into
and out of
weather. How
sight splinters
vision, braces me
here—there.
From a swamp
where the road
dead ends
life spools up
into un-
spooling
July haze.
A blue line
and a gray line.

A Title For the Haze

In a patch of sunlight
a decapitated grasshopper
twitches. The sunlight twitches.
Sky the size of a sky imagined.

Squint to see the quarter moon
—shallow gash on blue horizon.
Squint to hear beyond windows
wafting muzak. I'm half-awake

in this field of turned-on particulars.
A wreck of yellow blossoms
under a barn door window.

A barn door without the barn.

Curtains

No silence
in the house.

No house
in silence.

Something's
always

mumbling,
stridulating

into dust—
the drift

of it—
which is

not a
song.

On Migration

A split glyph
drags south
over a parking lot.

The suction
of dusk.
We watch it

wrest
margin
from margin.

Your face
in the half-light.

The aphasia
of the shape

of your face
in the half-light.

Autumn
embalms
the hour.

Take Place

It must be enough
to live in the variations

of wind alone.
To sing the seams.

Apprehended
by vision, we
think we've seen.

*

Gutted Sunday glow divided
by white and yellow
lines. Glass

crushed over asphalt—
the sparkle in a pothole.

No ideas
but in parking lots.

*

Grief ground down
to the bare sense of an I
imagining itself here.

Winter-chipped sidewalk
annotated by grass clippings

and bird shit
white as paint.

Phrase after phrase
falls into place, out of
place, rewriting a world.

Sight: a lengthening fracture.

*

A palette stammers
to assemble the landscape.

Rain claps
dead leaves.

In overgrown brush
a nameless animal's
short-circuited shriek.

*

A lucid dream
signals the new season.

All those flowering trees
rooted to graves.

*

Thin indentations
where language was—

toppled row of tombstones—

appear and reappear
under a long wave of grass.

*

When weather
won't say

the unsaid.
An exchange

between light and wind—

the way I'd want
a line to move
to carve space.

Light and wind,

and the objects
between them,

pronouncing
only themselves.

*

Between sidewalk and curb
tiger lilies flare and bend

—a shape that resembles
the shape of the thought
that found them
there.

*

As if a field guide
could prevent
the present

from disintegrating
around us.

*

Gasoline and honeysuckle
unravel the air. Air charged

with stridulation, echo-

location, what scatters at dusk
to scavenge and be scavenged.

*

The world is real
in its absence of a world.

Polar Low

Half-sheathed in ice
a yellow double-wide trailer

mirrors the inarticulate morning.
The amnesiac sun.

And nothing else
to contrast these variations of white

and thicket
choked by thicket

in thin piles that dim the perimeter.

Every other noun
frozen over.

Contain

Those concatenated
husks of ice
that line the lawn's
edge, far-
lapping shadows
(narrow, as if
scratched into
week-old
snow's scum-
pocked surface).
Give the day
its sign, some
emblem, to
read our-
selves out
of past
into place. No
world without
delineation. No
thing until
detonated
into its word.
Carpenter ant
navigates a knot
on an elm stump
and vanishes
through a cavity

of rot. Sight
is lost to sight.
At the border
between seasons
air's grainy with
light's lengthening.
Listen to an hour
shift shape, how
it contains
sonic detritus
in a dream-thin
frame, slush
spun under tires,
a church bell's
high note
bent above
dusk folding
the corners in.

Gauge

The color
of a thing
after it thaws
—raw, rusted.
April, a panic

pulls the field
apart, maps
the day in mud.
Long ruts of mud

and coruscated
edges where
runoff (so red
it's black) reflects
the sun-drift. There

flashes—here.
A wasp lands
on the page,

an unwritten phrase.

Illocality

To imagine a morning

the first
sounds from the street

and the house, its halls

scarifying
consciousness

Antique glass
smudges limbs

(more blue
than green)

flared out
over a roof

To imagine
the raw circumference

of a field
as it wakes

what we make of it

where our senses
send us

*

Gray oscillates gray
and the mountain

a line
lodged within it

gone slack at the end

*

No need
to mention
weather

The yard—
the measure

An unkempt
garden bed
convulses

synchronous
with traffic

flashing through
the fence

*

Stone bench
in a ring of weeds

Shadows ring—
a sound

Bees doused in
viscous sun,
erased

from *A New Silence*

For the Margin

Night leaves in its wake
a voice I don't recognize;
an echo flagging
in cold, bent
by cold

and the dull thud
of a 40 watt bulb.

At the seam
of panic
dawn erodes
the hour

while I wait for you,
the nameless,
to pronounce
the hollow

of what I'm not—

the poem
you already are.

The Reprieve

A week
that freezes, thaws,
and freezes again.

The skyline scales
and cracks.
Morning's frayed

gray plumes
pull through the wreck
and the wreck in mind.

To be reminded
there's grace
in ordinary weather,

in the reprieve
from neon
and clouds low enough

to cloud thought. Grace
in daylight, the drowse
and sway;

and how, when it's this
thin, things barely cling
to their names. Grace

to be nameless, a form
among forms, drifting
in January glare.

Grace, too,
when windows
reflect and distort,

at night,
the shape of a room.

Present Conditions

Today the weather within
is the weather without.
Even the wind is broken,
stammering over gnarled stalks
and black bulbs punctured through
snowpack. I'm alive
in the contrast, dragging myself
from a dream, eyes adjusting
to the bright. In a semaphore
of stripped limbs
the sun, segmented, multiplies.

Late March

And the mud again
ripped open

at the seams, silver
in afternoon's glowering

shine. Sunday
slowly implodes

into itself: the hollow
of a vowel humming

under the surface
we strain to pull

our voice—
a voice—through.

We've endured
a certain dormancy

and arrived in time
(out of time) to say it.

To imagine we've
said it, that it

could be enough.

Vigil

A contrail arcs
over the wreck. Snowbanks
returned to gravel; litter
and its language
ground to grit. This excuse
for spring. Nothing to see
beyond a blind spot
collapsing into afterimage.
Nothing to hear beyond a voice
consuming itself in an alley.
How the world expands
as a thought expands
with the angle of the season.
Between parking block
and dumpster
crocuses clarify
their square of shade.

Otherwise

Posthumous in spring, I

collapse into other
rhythms, colors

—a palette unspooled

at the speed of
dreaming. Forsythia

webs each edge
and edgeless gap

of a condemned home.
A row of them

strained into a season
where I stand

ahead of where
I stood, the shell

of a word,
of the air,

of what was
or wasn't said.

Temple

A tree as thin
as your wrist

sprays
from the split

in a river rock.

Brookside

The air, the dull glow of humidity; gnats and flies fray the corners, flash peripherally. Peeper chants pump from the other side of the brook, their dark pocket. When we stop talking, nothing else does. When language leaves us, how many other languages drum from the margins to reorganize the silence.

•

The world is what exceeds the capacity of our senses—the unseen momentum—this bright spillage ringing the day.

•

Pollen-skinned pond's edge by the dock where we stood and tried to describe it—as yellow as the memory of yellow, a memory of light without context. We gave up and just looked. And walked further.

On the Solstice

Lightning stilts
the gloam, lingers
behind the eyes.
A negotiation

between stasis
and abrasion,
petrichor
and car exhaust,

lends the weather
its broken music.
At dusk, I move
through the room

or the room moves
through me.
Night falls
into insect static.

Air too thick to think.
And the moon
in a pool
on old linoleum.

An Offering

Candle flame flinches
against the breath
I forgot I was breathing,
caught in August's exhale.
To see a thing clearly, listen
to the silence it inhabits.
Listen as traffic translates rain
into an open syllable
stretched toward the horizon.
Sit still in a still room
and watch weather pixelate
a window. Watch orange roses
in a makeshift vase
wilt on the sill.
This, too,
is a form of devotion.

Nothing More

Clover mite crushed
        under my finger, red
streak dragged over a blank
        page, as blank
as the hour, the day,
        despite the low hum
in the apartment:
        refrigerator motor
kicking on, the old man
        across the hall talking
to himself. It isn't enough
        to write into this
vacancy, to say
        the day's blank—
but what else is summer:
        what doesn't heat hollow
and reduce to a streak—
        these blown husks
striking pavement,
        a wasp trapped
between panes of glass.
        Leave the page stained.
A book of stains.
        The room dissolving
around a bolt of sun
        slashed down the wall.

Clear

After eight days of rain
what isn't overwritten
under sun. These

asphalt cracks
pushed further apart.
Eight days without

definition: gray walled
the room in, and I
thought I found a way

to stop thinking—to allow
gray to become a sound
I couldn't hum myself out of.

All I heard was a window.
A long weed beat
unevenly against it.

The Work

Summer is a ritual of endurance. The way rain rewinds into haze no color cuts through. Even the tiger lillies surrounding the supermarket parking lot are washed out, mute. Today's forecast: suffocation. You have to strain to catch the signal that ignites the voice flowering beyond the brain—a language you hardly know as your own, but it is yours. You stand outside the poem, tend to its edges. Worry the seams. Keep it from collapsing. This is the work you've been given. A power line in the fog, sloping toward infinity.

The Practice

Panic, the speechless
hour, blooms
in dust—

a spent web
vibrating
in a corner.

Where am I
without a word
to hold against
the day,

to witness
transparency
as prayer
and ballast.

Afternoon dark
as late dusk.
I listen
to thunder

hollow
the particular
silence of hail

raining
against glass.

My mind
finally removed
from the room

dissolves
in outside sound.

Garden Level

Night gives nothing back; it only appears to cohere. What's locked in dissolves without pause. An animal rattles mulch and twice-dead leaves piled against the window. I know the walls are there for the sounds they sift into the room—the room that inhabits me—underground.

*

Sun in the shape of a quadrangle on a wood floor. Curtains blown horizontal split it in half. Dust divots air, dents the pale afternoon. An hour isn't like anything, not even itself. A window, a patch of lawn, a street for the tide of its noise, for measure. A stream of particulars undoing the room.

*

It can take all day to filter out the debris of a dream, to see a thing contained by its terms. Call it clarity. You have to almost stop thinking; get up to the edge of the clanging at the back of the brain. Go dumb to the light.

*

Three weeks in and the season begins to click. Weather to word; word to weather. A bird circles, punctuates a bloodless sky—the husk we're under. The street a monochrome stream. Cold enough to numb thought.

*

Snow light at dusk, the deepening bruise; a blue that hums. A soundless ringing between the eyes where all things sink and disperse. For once we're reading the world without the names by which we dream it. Nothing to say; nothing saying us.

★

Everything comes to a point along the horizon; every limb stripped to a line. Even the clouds sharpen, shaved against a mountain. A pond duplicates the scene—if your gaze drops. To suspend the senses in the drone of geometry. To forget the traffic here.

★

The way the mind bends to receive injured weather, the sudden warmth, as though half awake and watching a place—a room, a field—assemble itself one object at a time. A syntax expanding beneath fanned rays of gaping sun. Center everywhere, circumference nowhere.

Placeholder

Now that the animal
trapped in the rafters

is silent, the cold alone

is a sound.
February's glare

bent by Victorian glass

casts the outline
of a spike of ice

spread from floor to ceiling—

the only thing
holding the house up.

Northern Tracks

Ferns flash dark,
chafe train windows
relieved by graffiti:
faded white runes
scrawled on
an underpass slant.
Barbed-wire fence
wrapped around
cracked concrete,
crabgrass, green
plastic bags
ballooning light.
A sign reads
SPECIAL METALS
as we coast into
a ghost town—
half a ghost,
at least, lingering.
Every window
in every building
broken—one
with a branch
lanced into it.
Tree and house
fused, as if
attached
to the same

decaying root
system. A freight
train passes
in the opposite
direction, loaded
with fertilizer:
green and white
sacks stacked and
blurred into blue
that looks
like memory,
a memory
barely there,
washed out—
still enough
to sting. How
sight stings when
things scroll
at this speed;
particulars
particlized.
Yellow sweep
of brown,
of black,
of summer
that hasn't
released into
fall. First
day of fall,
today—

muggy and
bright. But
the air's
hollow edge
foreshadows
October. Now
the car's
flanked by
factories
in pieces
weeds and
abandoned
mattresses
cinch together.
It's true: Nothing's
uninhabited.
Nothing
goes un-
reclaimed. Red
leaves radiate
in dense brush
bordering woods.
Red sticks
to my peripheral
vision,stains it,
while highway
streaks horizon:
red striations
thread the glare.
Slow, close

to a station.
Algae skirts
a brick wall's
bent reflection
where pond
meets mud,
knotted brush,
roots buckled
aboveground.
The view opens—
opening completely
to the Connecticut
River; the surface
wrinkling what's
left of the day.

After Trakl

When weather gives permission to forget

When the outline of the field reels like a flame and folds in

When the mountains rust into a past-tense sky;

        horizon dim as memory

When October gloam corrals in an alley and I

        sift it for a phrase

to contain night, to cloak the mind quiet

When voices overwhelm the dark overwhelming the room

When all I'll know of summer, soon, is a tone gone hollow

        —a sun too small to see

A Window in New England

Noun by noun dusk draws
down night, a singular thing-
lessness, an open
syllable pronouncing lack.
How breath alone becomes sight.

*

Call it November—
the mountain carved flat by fog;
the bottomed-out clouds
refusing metaphor, no
language left to contain them.

*

This morning the light
is bleached by cold. Pinhole sun
caught up in clear quartz.
Blinded, I read the quiet
unwriting frost, field, fence, gull.

★

Church bells bend into
syllables, into patterns:
these leafless shadows
on the lawn clawing toward
asphalt, dispersing the day.

★

Now the room contains
the season, its signs inscribe
the wall, ink their way
across. When wind litters air
the lines vibrate—the room moves.

★

A silence beyond
mind, beyond thought. The way air
and light hum soundless-
ly over a field patched with
frost. The way vision listens.

*

Call it December—
skyline abbreviated
by a rogue cloud deck.
Dead leaves rattle through traffic.
Another world closes in.

*

Nothing to pronounce
but morning's disorder. What
the dark sifts into
light: the room and its corners—
this illegible shadow.

*

On the cusp of June
the sun's already August.
Peripheral bees
at the speed of memory
indent the humidity.

*

Half the mountain drenched
in cloud shadow, the other
green as a thought of
green, an afterthought of green,
the green that remains of green.

*

Rain that wasn't fore-
casted streaks the afternoon
blind, a blurred version
of a world we imagine
we haven't imagined there.

*

Distracted by hail
strafing the window, I lost
the silence centered
between my eyes. But silence—
listen—has nowhere to go.

*

There is no poem
if the breath doesn't tether
to a phrase, suspend-
ing the day in its silence,
collapsing time to a word.

*

As if Niedecker
were a verb: her chiseled breath,
how it palpitates
the page. To find company
in silence turning a phrase.

*

How morning coheres
even as a dream repeats
behind my open
eyes: paper blinds leak light, un-
write the dark that gripped the room.

*

Cid said poverty's
a gift, the ground and the grist
for poetry. Cid
was wrong. How does anyone
catch enough breath from nothing?

*

After how many
days spent in fluorescent light,
a spray of lilacs
scars my vision while I walk
around the chapel garden.

*

Almost August, heat
hangs breath-heavy wherever
we walk, even shade
suffocates thought, and language—
this nonsense syllable—wilts.

*

It isn't these name-
less flowers unfolding from
a narrow alley,
it's the weeds, long and knotted,
that give their rhythm to shade.

*

Pond's edge pocked white with
cottonwood fluff. Wind-scattered
litter drifts: a spent
condom lost now in pollen—
sluggish current curving green.

*

There's no metaphor
here. The sky in the pothole
is the sky I see—
I write to say I've seen it.
Long clouds suspended in oil.

*

Out of the air of
the page—to draw enough breath—
to speak quietly
so that you might mishear me—
and hold the poem open.

*

Allow the poem
to do your breathing for you—
and forget the breath
in the wake of a language
you know now to be your own.

*

The gift is to wake
nameless, wordless, without form
in a room without
walls, the shapeless bright, the breath
cleaving a self from silence.

*

Summer's brushed light laps
through the chapel. The last light
before dusk. Above
a small altar, in shadow,
a locked tabernacle rests.

*

A shock of rain-dark
irises rising from brick—
a fallen wall. How
many hours later, the
color still caught in my throat.

from *Rosary Made of Air*

Breath Work

i.

Even if there were a world
it wouldn't bother to be ours.
We know the mind is better left lost

and each thing it feigns to anchor.
It's enough to just sit—
to breathe each other here,

awake in what language lacks,
while a jagged line of late gulls

vanishes into a low cloud
that says snow but doesn't

ii.

Snow plows vibrate the walls
and the water in a vase shakes:
flowers that fail
to fool my room away from winter

sit on a speaker blaring news:
panic sapped into fatigue.
I navigate the day
through windows, shadows

barring the floor; I track the season
by what sticks to sewer grates.
Today they're under half a foot of snow.
I'm walking in it, hungover, hovering

over a notebook to chisel a phrase.
Sky's gray grain gathering white.
White enclosing white.
A clean and marginless page.

iii.

Sunday is the ritual of Sunday
repeating its name
until it disintegrates.
What remains: half-dead
grocery store flowers
losing blue petals on the altar.

And this thoughtless sense of light lengthening
despite the darkness in the room.

iv.

Memory's a husk hung to dry
in sunbeams latticed over a parking lot
snowbank. Crushed Coke can
lodged at the peak.

A shadow that would claim me
rocks on its heels by a pile of slush;
but the weather is heavier
than superstition,
and I am unburdened.

I is a husk, a witness,
mere consciousness
navigating the edge
of the cusp
of spring.

V.

After death-deep sleep
I wait for the day's first omen.

Skinned black branches
wind lashes between clouds
that make the mountain small.

The mountain still snowed over
even after last night's rain. White

creased russet with traprock. This
is the counterpoint to the wind

and what it can't articulate, this
stone holding the horizon down.

vi.

At dusk starlings roost
in the belfry of a closed
Catholic church. Wood
warped by how many winters—
too soft to throw an echo.

vii.

First few signs of spring
and mania animates

the dormant corners.
What my mind cannot contain

the field contains—the light shakes.

Clouds stacked in Robert
Lax stanzas disperse behind

the mountain—a kind
of vapor now—a blue plume

the sun pulls further apart.

viii.

Mountain made bald
by a microburst.

Ridge stubbled
with new growth

stilts the cloud veil.
I'll sit

until the last patch of snow
dissolves into stone.

ix.

Spring coming in, coming on.

March is mud
and bright dusk,
liminal and littered; a pause
before forsythia, honeysuckle,
alleys overwhelmed with weeds.

Roots breathe beneath receding snow.

x.

Cold rain claws dusk. I
close the window and listen.
The perfect poem
is without words, is the thing
itself thoughtlessly ringing.

Manifesto

i.

Poetry's enough
to sustain
the day.
Sliced June light
fills a crystal
vase sitting
on a sill's
cracked white
paint: emptiness
brimming over
a name, bloom-
ing into shadow.

ii.

Nothing other
than now—
than this—

white moth
navigating
honeysuckle

coiled around
a wrought iron
handrail.

iii.

Notice
the breath.
And when it

lengthens
watch the mind
unspool

into pond water
repeating
clouds.

iv.

In June's lucid dream
rain blurs a world
into focus

and the poem appears
where it always was—

before you.

v.

The sound of the pencil
writing the sound
of the rain.

The Shape of Something Said

No time beyond daylight
waving on the floor

like spilled water, and so it goes.
This window won't hold

the omens that pass. My mind
haunts my body as my body

haunts the room
and there's a glitch

in the quiet, an inked-in echo.
Sleep is a relief.

Sleep and poetry.
Not words, but the space

around words
anchors me to an hour.

Across the street
forsythia bursts from black rubble.

Even inside, I'm surrounded
by what wakes in April.

No time beyond shadows
spilled around windows.

A nameless tree's makeshift sundial
sliding deeper into the mulch.

Late Time

The weather is panic
evaporated into gusts

of cold sun. White sun
cracking gray clouds

bulked low
on the horizon.

What am I
but an animal

lumbering
through a late time

waiting for
an impossible spring,

waiting for
the mind to settle,

for static to sink
beneath song.

I wait for relief.
I wait for the heart

to open, for
the voice to thaw.

And sparrows,
how do they survive

hollow-boned
in an arctic blast?

Yesterday's news:
wet confetti

scattered over
curbside slush.

Cold, white sun
lands across my face

as I turn a corner;
and I am weightless

without a name,
nameless without

a form, dissolved
into particulars

unspooled into
consciousness,

unwinding
into a world

never more
than now.

Keepsake

The friend who betrayed
me, I hold no malice
toward him, remembering when
we drove the backroads
of Western Massachusetts,
and wild turkeys, barely lit by what red
remained of a sunset, crossed the road
and we stopped to let them pass.
We stopped talking, after hours
of talk, and watched those ghosts,
those turkey-shaped shadows,
slowly cross a narrow road
into woods where it was already night.

Poem Against Cancellation

Vow to see
what isn't
immediately
seen, what
takes time
to sift
into view;
takes time
and keeps time
as the gift
of a space
in which
to perceive
the inverse
of surface,
and to know
the world
is many—
many worlds
within.
No voice
is single—
a tapestry
of history
and pitch—
and to hear it
is to receive it

without
surrendering
to an impulse
to destroy it.
Say the un-
kempt shrub
is full of bees
and bees
weave sun
through a new
season. Say
there's no account-
ing for the world
and how it
defies
a frame. Say
within the one—
within you—
infinities
flourish.

To a New Friend

Daylight disassembles into sound—
the hum I hold in my head
is the hum you hold in your head, too.
The poem, written or unwritten,
is enough to see us through the thaw.

Soon the fields will fill with names.

Mud will rupture with indescribable color.

Satori in Easthampton

The sun crests over Family Dollar. I narrow my sight to see spring's debris drift across the parking lot. Dandelion seed heads sheathe wind. The shape of the wind; the grain of the light. Today there's joy in the blur. To seize time by saying what surrounds me, when words instantly slip from the surfaces they feign to reflect. As if language were an anchor and not a kind of scar tissue. Today there's joy in the voice that falters to locate me here.

September 8th, 2021

Poetry went cold
this summer.

The days
wouldn't translate

into a phrase.
The world

was what reached
through the weather

I was under.
My mind mirrored

a room
vibrating at night

in cricket-dense quiet.
All that's left

of summer:
a cloud deck skims

the top
off a mountain

and a sun-bleached
lottery ticket

snagged by prongs
of Russian sage

tongues
the chlorinated air.

Altar and Offering

i.

Through November's
arterial horizon
traffic flickers.
Mountain bare

but for a bent cloud
clipping the ridge.
What would it mean
to see clearly—

to know
nothing's there
other than what is.

ii.

A clearing
between scrub
and birches peeling

(white sheets flagging)
where sunset sparks.

And those hollow tones:
geese gathered at the river's
gravel bank.

They're not singing;
they're sounding out

a sequence of notes
describing the color
and shape of the cold.

iii.

The poem begins without a word
while I walk through sideways snow.

Snow barbed by a gone season.

There's joy in the unsaid and how it accumulates.

This god-vacant pain, the run-on days, disrupted.

iv.

The day before
the longest night

of the year,
December sun

snags runoff
from last week's

snowfall—
a silver cord binding

my eyes to asphalt,
traffic, dead leaf

floating in the flash.
Overnight rain

rearranged
the mountain:

white to red,
faint red

pulse
under russet.

Blinded again,
I'm rooted

to a world
without me.

Wordless prayer
—this vacancy

where the new life begins.

v.

Streetlight
suspends hail
in a sepia orb.

The fricative hiss
as stripped trees
sift it. I hear it

as language
refusing
to become speech.

A circular breath
extinguishing
the familiar.

vi.

Open the blinds
to snowlight—
that bright, particular pain.

There, in the shock,
locate the real

before it sinks
into synesthesia.

This is how winter
makes itself useful:

it tricks the body

to trick
the mind still.

vii.

Up late listening
to rain run ice

into mud.
Does the room
contain sound

or does sound
contain the room?

Walls dissolve
in the dark—
a locked door opens.

viii.

I covet the cold,

how it punctures
memory

and dislodges
the rot. When

wind
is enough—

harsh enough—
to smother thought.

ix.

Clouded
by snow fog

a snowed-over
mountain—mind

makes it
visible.

x.

After the snow squall
sun mutes
what snow remains
in my vision, and the figure

on the other side of the crosswalk

too bright to say

walking toward
or away from me.

xi.

A few days lost
to a false spring.
Black slush caged
by bolts of light.

My mind, jolted,
turned jagged;
but last night
the cold returned

and when I woke
morning was a window
in the shape of a field
draped in frozen fog.

xii.

A vulture circles
a shotgun's echo, carving

into cloudless sky
the shape of the field below.

The air alone
both altar and offering.

On the Cusp

i.

Time condenses
beyond me; the lines
hold a whole season.
Signs by which to see
when false weather
blurs the real. How
this God-quiet husk—
what waits to be said—
lights the dark
swarming toward us.

ii.

Underground, I trace
the changing season
by texture alone. Beams
of sidelong sun cut
through a thin slit of glass;
they brace the floor
beneath me
and move slowly
to hold the table to my hand.

iii.

The way the light grows
viscous, gold
around the edges.
This hazy levitation of grief.
To begin again—
anointed by Your silence—
when August was all I thought I knew.

iv.

Alive, finally, in the afterlife
of summer, I walk home
in the gloaming, and the mind
stops chiming. When panic
exhausts itself the colors
return, the world returns:
Orange bending into red, yellow
blending into lavender sweeping
the horizon, punctured by white
headlights. The gift is given. I walk
and watch my hand rock
in its own shadow like a bell.

v.

As the days narrow
and shadows lengthen, burrow
in words that cast light
before night consumes the room
and dead leaves rattle windows.

vi.

Outside of the window
snow devils rise
and unwind
in horizontal snowfall.
I read the glass, a wordless
book. Wordless, but full of
phrases—motion and texture.
An outline of silence
filled in by silence.

vii.

I walk to channel an hour
away from pain,
face in full-blasted sun.
January sun—sudden, startles
the mind quiet. Swallows lift off
all at once from the power line
and the sound is singular, a gasp,
a sheet of thick paper torn fast.

viii.

I wander through
the shell called winter.
Hollow wreck of stripped limbs
where the sun, small now, droops.
Mindless blessing—
the gift of consciousness.
I'm stranded in a body
that barrels beyond me,
splayed white rays
distorting my vision.

ix.

To navigate pain
with language alone.
The language of the dead
cuts a moment close
and time collapses.
I'm alive in the company.
"Urge and urge and urge…"
The heart settles, held
by breath breaking
into sound, my body
merging into words.

The Turn

Awake in the pre-dawn dark
at the end of a difficult year,

I gather scraps from a notebook
to contain grief
in private speech.

The words repeat like a rosary:

sun, silence, time,
light, day, pain.

As if ink could snare a voice
beyond me—for company—

and dissolve the "I"
in an image
at once blurred and vivid.

That was the vow and the dream.

Morning, bright now
between the margins—

cloud, window,
sparrow, rain—

at the end of a difficult year.

The Walk

At dusk, the lamps
flick on behind windows—

that spectral,
amber glow—
and I'm dizzy

with nostalgia
for an almost forgotten dream.

At dusk, shadows deepen

before they fade,
engraved

in asphalt
and old snow
slumped like ash against a curb.

I hold my hands to my face
and breathe into my palms:
Thank God.

Thank God
for the freezing wind—

my mind stops.

Removed

Another faceless
season. Eyes pass
narrowed by fear

and hollow
in the lull
of language
lost
to hell.

To survive:
marvel
at the unraveling
of a world
that was never
yours.

Wake early.

Allow
the soundless hours
to wash over

and become
the poem.

from *The Light of No Other Hour*

Soma

I spent spring half-tethered
to a body that was and wasn't
mine. The form was familiar, but I
dangled beyond it. Was it
the mind, the thing that buzzed—
a sound straining to become
language, caught between blades of light
outshining a flowering pear tree.
I'm whole in summer's monotone;
I'm flesh in this heat.
I think through this body,
alive on a Friday, on a bench,
watching a wasp dodge traffic.
A wasp dissolving into chalk-white sun.

Intercession

What's real
remains blurred
until we say
its name. Lord,
keep me tethered.
Grief burns
in my throat, but
morning slants
into a new season.
Pear trees
flower along
both sides of
the street
and flex
with wind,
off-white
and pixelated
like lungs
breathing memory
or a frame
from a dream
dissolving
before a shock of
forsythia spikes
the landscape yellow.
The colors flood
through me,

what's left of me
in the sudden
absence of thought.
Call it happiness.
Call it the center
of a prayer.
What's left of me
when the images
pour in
like a chant
or a charm
and scatter
into the seamless.
To see
by means
of the unseen.
Lord, keep me
tethered
to meaning:
Your silence
where all things
are holy.
All things
vibrating with
light, April
light. Light
with no winter
left in it. Light
of no other hour.

Spear Thistle

The heat seals
the day beneath
a sheet of faded sepia.

Summer is bardo—
gnat-flecked and feral.

Still, I covet wakefulness
in this season of sleep and the odd wildflower.

Closer to October

Potholes full of rings
of rain ex-
panding, vanishing

into each other.
Gone, lost in
these infinities,

I walk the seam where
summer with-
draws. Cold rain devoid

of even a trace
of August.
Rust on the maples

and on the Kousa
dogwoods: red
berries beaming through

the gathering gloam.

Far

Your silence
is as full
as anything spoken

or sung,
or found far
in October-deep

limbs
patterned
around a pond

I thought was a lake
for the landscape
of color reflected—

the crowded
maples, embers
in waves.

Deep November

Fog droops
over a narrow creek.

Limbs shook bare
claw their reflection

into brackish water
lapping a retainer wall

stained with blue graffiti.
What the heart can't hold

the mind churns into static
the day alone decodes.

But the wind—
the first syllable of winter—

needles my face numb
and my hands, numb,

raise up an absence.

Found Poem

for Jacqueline, in memory

i.

    When we visited
Dickinson's grave our
shadows crossed the stone—
    crossed out "CALLED
BACK." What else was there
    to say or to see.

ii.

    This is translation,
this is poetry,
the alchemy in
        a word—in
death—you continue
        to pronounce yourself.

iii.

    I imagine you
wanted, finally,
to be free from words—
       in the rain
ghost-pale petals drift
      beyond metaphor.

iv.

    The space between lines—
horizon on top
of horizon, where
    you wait for
meaning to rise from
    silence—a small sun.

v.

    Fat bees vault between
blossoms, loop through light
the wind can't contain—
       winter gone
in colors flooding
      the margin of you.

vi.

    Nameless, wordless light,
this is what remains
of you: the outline
       of a dream
drawn deeper into
     dawn—into morning.

vii.

    And now you're nowhere
being everywhere
at once, found and un-
        found, without
language to brace you
      from becoming earth.

Before Mass

After a night
wracked with panic,

it's a gift to sit
in the center
of a motionless hour.

    Stained-glass
glazing vacant pews.

Pilgrim

On the Feast Day of St. Benedict Joseph Labre

Emptied of the world,
you walked the earth

(God-gone
and God-given)

in an undertow
of prayer.

In a crown of gnats
you swooned

and slept.
Saint,

on your feast day
when the rain passed

a dozen potholes
held a dozen suns.

Saint Brigid's

Gravestones, nameless
after a century of weather—

shadows stream
narrow-limbed

over uneven ground.
Summer's first murmur:

gnats and honeysuckle
cloud the cemetery's

night-green edge—
green throbbing

and slowly tumbling in.
I sit

with the stones
until silence

abides silence.
Mercy.

How we're all always turning
back into earth.

Prayer Walk

At summer's brink,
yellow forsythia haze
dissipates into thunder

and petrichor. Spring
was a memory
of spring.

Bone-thin trees
drift from their roots
in a ditch filled with dark weeds.

Peepers quaver
and go on quavering—
the sound the mind makes

when panic
seizes thought.
But tonight the mind is still,

cinched to silence
by syllables
vibrating through

a loop of beads.

a broken line of
geese rowing
silently through snow

Beads

i.

A dream
disintegrates
into a room—

my body
made of
light.

ii.

I don't notice
until I'm surrounded,

my senses seized
by the season.

Leaf-tides
sidewind
asphalt;

color clots
sewer grates.

iii.

The flare
and the fire
bright before
dying—

November's
quick
turn
inward

turns
the mind
inside-out.

iv.

Freezing air
cuts through
closed windows,
encapsulating pain.

The poem glows
unwritten
in the center of
the room.

V.

An inner-silence
blots out nostalgia.

What was left
unspent
in autumn
withers
under ice.

Now the new life;
the holy order

of dawn breaking.

vi.

First, the maples turn.
Embers fill the field.

The maples turn
before the mind turns

to face the season.
What would it mean

for October
to think through me?

Give myself over
to the rhythm

of things decaying?
These beads of wordless prayer

reeling in
the early dark.

Lux Brumalis

i.

Lately, poetry
and prayer
reconcile silence.

Collapsing
into dawn, you see
how night lacked
nothing—darkness spoke.

ii.

Abbreviated
days engrave
shadow into stone.

iii.

Red winter sunset—
even the pavement

in this vacant parking lot
softens under the color.

iv.

Windblown snow in sun—
a friend's voice
dissolving the ache.

v.

Gnarled limbs
grapple air—
air made visible

through undone
columns of snow.

vi.

The inaudible
syllable—
half moon in daylight.

vii.

Brittle syllables,
bitter prayer,

freezing air
held in my palms

as if to translate
the nameless.

viii.

Over thinning snow
shadows of
dead flowers flail.

Three Mornings in March

i.

At the seam
between sleep
and consciousness,
morning birds
and rain
mirror
the shape
of the room.

ii.

Through a snow squall, I
walked home and knew Your presence
in the visibly
invisible, and the sting
when the wind changed direction.

iii.

Here in the dying
world, in God's
sleep, geese
lift up

        and out
of the half-thawed pond.

Lenten Syllables

i.

This false spring, this un-
raveling sorrow, O God,
and these sparrows in
a mangled shrub, how they form
a body—head gone in song.

ii.

After a false spring
when the sun returns to dust
and the clouds are dust,
the geese—pulled into a point—
puncture dull and blinding gray.

iii.

Gone white overnight,
the mountain presses into
hovering gray sky.
Geese in the shape of a snapped
arrow—chant echoing chant.

iv.

As the ashen snow
melts, gutters become dream-blurred
mirrors reflecting
wire-thin branches scrawled across
traffic and a dying sun.

v. (Coda)

A voice in the night   the sound of snow
falling through snow   a voice thin with prayer
and winter   and a memory of light
perforated by spring   the sound of snow
whirling around streetlights   an imagined sound
honed by the cold and held in mind   a voice
in the night that needs no response
beyond acknowledgment   the listening
this leaning in to decipher precisely nothing.

Unseasonably

i.

Spring coming in now, in the light, in these scintillated edges when it touches a thing, and returns things—say, the dormant globe thistle, rows of faded gravestones, the ragged sparrow perched on a chain-link fence—to their names. We catch our breath and wait. Tomorrow, snow.

ii.

The delirium of spring: colors emerging, margins blurred. Wind spinning bright shackles over the pond before dispersing into a warped reflection of the sky. In this weather, I walk a half-step beyond my body. In this weather, I practice death. Pale, carbonated light, within which all things from a distance appear to levitate.

iii.

April's unrecognizable. Each breeze a husk of summer's bloodlessness. Insects the size of a fist. No, the heart can't catch up, torn into sepia grief. Every wild and nameless thing mindlessly reaching. I look for you in the blur—a face to anchor my mind in the real.

iv.

Some color returns. Incandescent green horizon. Listen to frogs trill deep in the brush, and know it is spring. A flowering pear tree flickers white through a ragged curtain of rain. A swallow cuts against the current and vanishes. This is the sacrament of the present moment. Time passes through the body, leaving a poem in the mouth.

The Last Poem

It is enough
to be nothing,
porous
to what appears.
It is enough

to sit on a bench
and watch a contrail
dissolve into dust,
to make a day of it.

It is enough
to look
in order to see,
and to know
there's a difference.

It is enough
to walk myself awake
in sub-zero wind,

snow-blind
and heartbroken.
It is enough
to forget.

It is enough
to borrow

from the dead
a voice

to sing through,
to survive the season.

It is enough,
the poems cramped
in the margins
of a water-stained
notebook—

leave them there
to be revised
by time.

It is enough—

alone
at the end of the year
engulfed by a presence
I am not compelled to name.

Acknowledgements

Thank you to the editors and publishers of
the books, chapbooks, journals, and broadsides
where many of the poems in this book first appeared.

ABOUT THE AUTHOR

Joseph Massey is the author of seven full-length
collections of poetry. He lives in the Pioneer Valley
of Massachusetts.

Follow his work online at www.poetrydispatches.com.

A NOTE ON THE TYPES

The main text of this book is set in Dante, designed
in 1952 by Giovanni Mardersteig and released in its
digital redrawn version in 1993 by Monotype. It is described by
no less a figure than Robert Bringhurst as 'one of
the great achievements of twentieth-century typography'.

Poem titles are in Avenir Next Regular,
Akira Kobayashi and Adrian Frutiger's reworking
of Frutiger's classic typeface Avenir; its clean lines
make an attractive pairing with
the dignity of Dante.

Made in United States
Orlando, FL
11 May 2024